A Gerbil For A Friend

by Donna Lugg Pape
illustrated by Diane Martin

Prentice-Hall, Inc., Englewood Cliffs, N.J.

jE
c. 1

Printed in the United States of America • J

Prentice-Hall International, Inc., London
Prentice-Hall of Australia, Pty. Ltd., North Sydney
Prentice-Hall of Canada, Ltd., Toronto
Prentice-Hall of India Private Ltd., New Delhi
Prentice-Hall of Japan, Inc., Tokyo

Library of Congress Cataloging in Publication Data

Pape, Donna (Lugg)
    A gerbil for a friend.

    SUMMARY: Briefly describes how Mark cares for and
tames his pet gerbil.
    1. Gerbils as pets—Juvenile literature.
[1. Gerbils as pets] I. Martin, Diane, illus.
II. Title.
SF459.G4P37   636'.93'233   73-4646
ISBN 0-13-353979-2

Mark has a small, furry pet. It's gentle and quiet. It's very clean too. Mark has a gerbil.

Mark calls his gerbil Lucy. Lucy fits right in Mark's pocket. She can leap out of it like a kangaroo. Her long tail helps her keep her balance. That's why some people call gerbils pocket kangaroos.

Mark knew Lucy's mother and father before Lucy was born. They live in a big cage in his classroom. The teacher took down the names of boys and girls who wanted a gerbil when Lucy's mother had babies. Mark's name was third on the list.

One morning, there were four new babies in the gerbils' cage. They were tiny and pink. Mark's teacher said they couldn't hear yet. Their eyes were still shut. "Squeak, squeak," they said, as they nosed around their mother.

Mark knew right away that Lucy
was the one he wanted. His
teacher marked her ear with a
drop of red food color so Mark
could be sure which one was
Lucy. She grew a little every day
and soon her pink body was
covered with brown fuzz.

George   Ed   Marge   Lucy

Her eyes opened and her teeth started to grow. When she was three weeks old, Lucy and her brothers and sister moved to another cage. They were being weaned and were learning to live without their mother. The teacher told Mark that he could take Lucy home in three weeks.

Mark needed to find a gerbil cage for Lucy. He took his father shopping for one. They looked at metal cages first. "But won't Lucy spill seed all over if she has this cage?" Mark's father asked.

"No," said the man in the pet shop. "You can put the cage inside a cardboard carton to catch the spill, like this." "What else do you have?" Mark's father asked. "We have plastic cages," said the man.

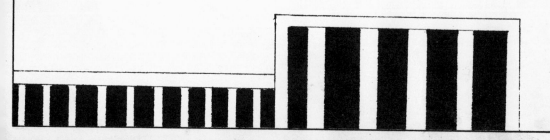

Mark's father thought the plastic cage was too expensive. "I can sell you an aquarium with a crack in it," the man said. Mark and his father liked that. There was enough money left to buy Lucy a water bottle.

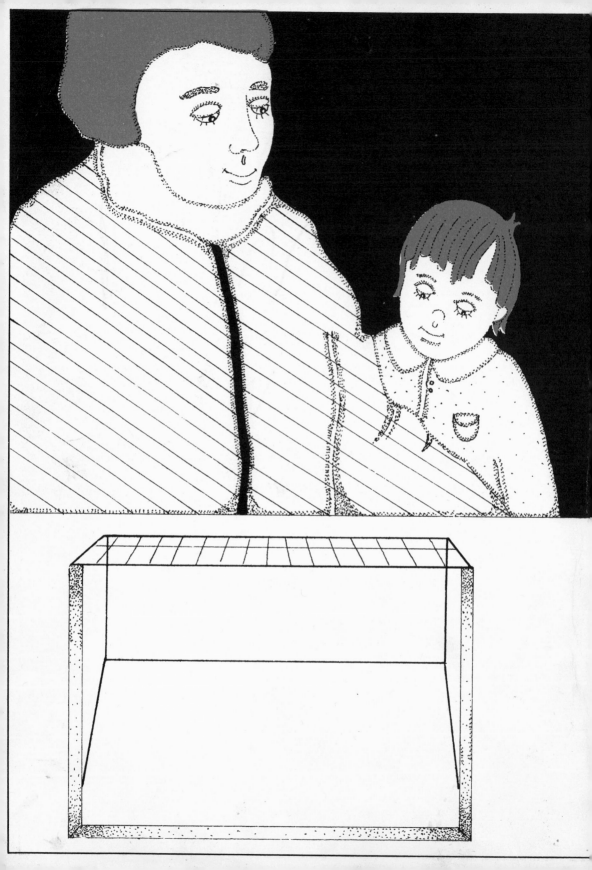

"This will be big enough," Mark's father said when they brought it home. "When Lucy is older and needs more room to jump, we will build her a cage ourselves." Then he covered the top of the aquarium with tough wire with the holes very close together. Mark put the cage out of the sunlight in his bedroom because the heat could kill Lucy. He covered the bottom of the cage with cedar shavings and tissue paper.

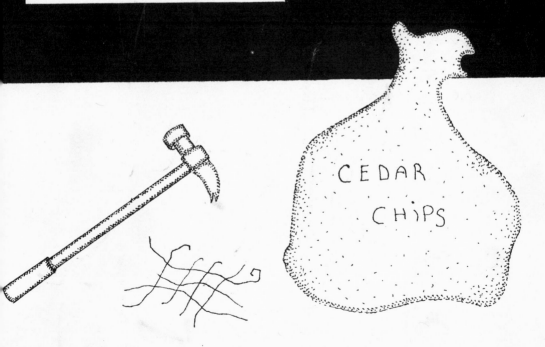

CEDAR
CHIPS

The day Lucy was to come home with him, Mark brought a shoe-box to school. He put Lucy inside it and tied a string around it. "Ta-ta-TAT," Lucy thumped with her foot. Gerbils do this when they are excited. Mark was excited too.

Mark didn't pick Lucy up for a whole day after he brought her home. Lucy needed a chance to get used to her new home. He watched Lucy burrow in her cedar shavings on the floor. Sometimes she burrowed so deep he couldn't see her. He watched her chew the tissue paper up for a nest. He watched her run.

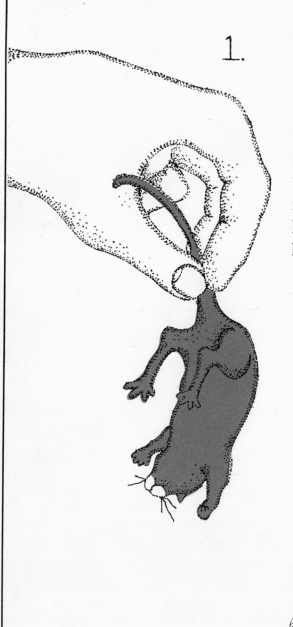

1.

Now Mark picks Lucy up a lot. He holds his hand like a cup. Then he places his hand under her and lifts. He also picks her up by the base of her tail. He never picks her up by the end of her tail because this could hurt her.

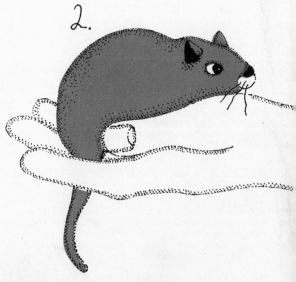

2.

Lucy's favorite food is sunflower seeds. Mark likes to watch Lucy eat a sunflower seed. She sits as a squirrel does, holding the seed in her front paws. She uses her sharp teeth to break the shell. Too many sunflower seeds are not good for Lucy.

Mark fed Lucy about two tea-spoons of hamster food that first day. Lucy also likes rolled oats birdseed, bread crusts and dry cereal. Now that she is older, he feeds her a tablespoon of food each day.

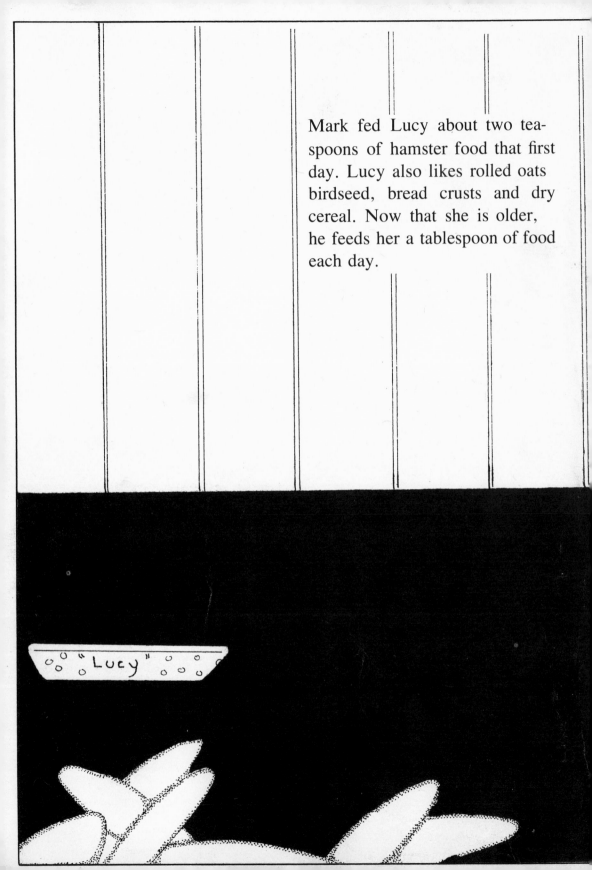

"Lucy"

Mark doesn't leave leftover
vegetables in Lucy's cage. He
throws them away before he gives
her new food. But he knows he
can put a lot of seed in the cage
at one time because gerbils
don't overeat.

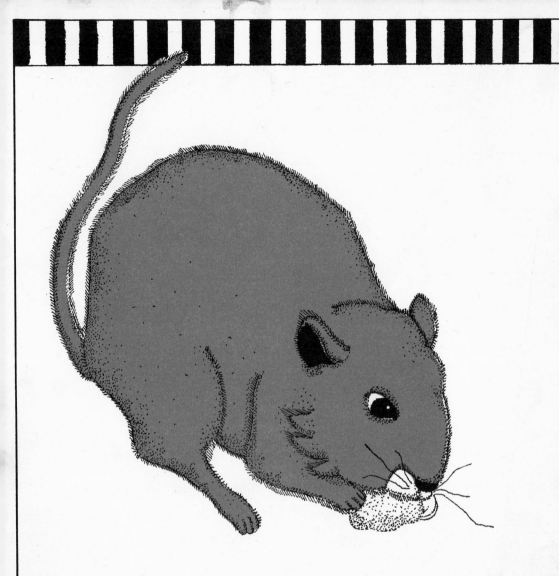

Besides dry food, a gerbil needs
a few greens. Mark feeds Lucy
greens about four times a week.
Too many greens could give her
a stomach-ache. Lucy likes
lettuce, raw carrots, and alfalfa.
She likes apples and oranges too.

Mark sometimes gives Lucy potato chips, pretzels, or crackers to eat—but only once in a while.

A gerbil is a very busy pet. When she is awake, Lucy is always doing something. She gets tired quickly. Then she takes a short nap.

Mark knows when Lucy is ready for a nap. She yawns and stretches. She likes to sleep curled up in a ball. Mark never wakes Lucy when she is napping. He knows this would make her very cross.

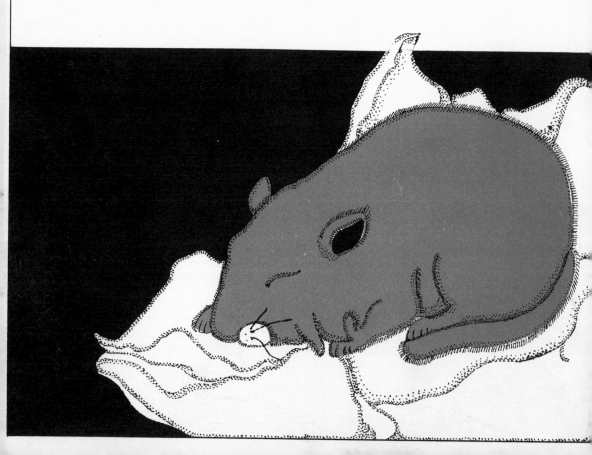

Lucy doesn't drink water very often. But Mark keeps a water bottle in her aquarium just in case she does get thirsty. Lucy stands on her hind legs to drink.

Lucy is so clean that Mark changes the cedar shavings only every two or three weeks. When it is time to clean Lucy's cage, Mark scrapes and sweeps it before covering the bottom with new cedar shavings. Sometimes Mark will have to scrub Lucy's home. He will air and dry it before he puts Lucy back inside.

Lucy keeps herself clean the same way a cat does. She washes herself with her tiny tongue.

Mark will put Lucy in the bath-tub while he cleans her cage. He knows Lucy can't leap high enough to get out of the tub. Of course, the tub will be dry. Gerbils don't like water very much.

Gerbils like to gnaw on things. This keeps their teeth from growing too long. If Lucy gets enough hard food, like rabbit pellets, her teeth will stay the right size.

Mark gives Lucy cardboard to gnaw on. Sometimes he gives her wood. Lucy would gnaw on her screen roof if she could get her nose through one of the holes. But the screen's holes are too small for Lucy's nose to push through. Lucy's nose could get hurt if the screen holes were larger.

Mark likes to have Lucy sit on his shoulder. He holds very still when she does this. Lucy likes to crawl up and down on Mark's arm. When Mark has a pocket, she is sure to crawl inside. Then she crawls right back out again.

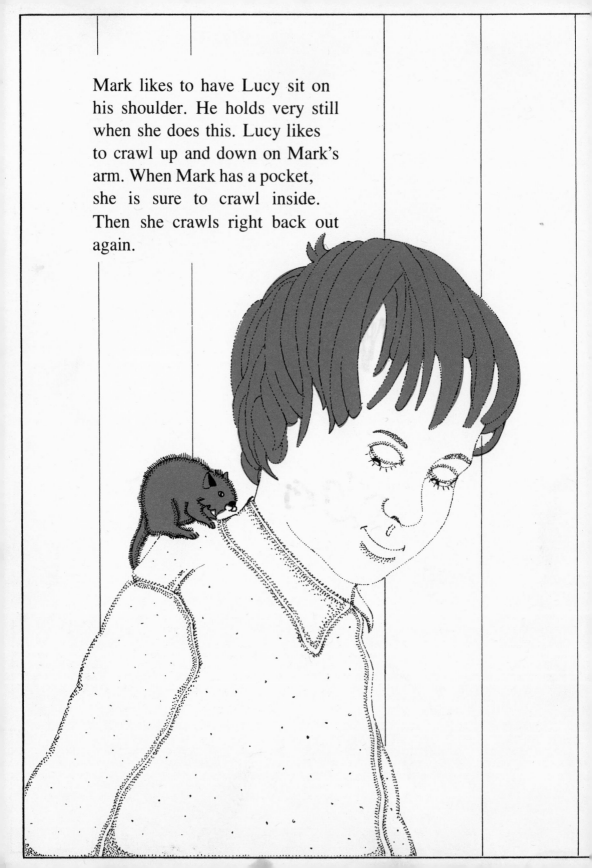

Running on a tabletop is fun for Lucy. Mark watches to make sure she doesn't get too close to the edge. Mark also gives Lucy cardboard tubes to run through.

Sometimes, Mark closes his bed-room door and lets Lucy run all around. It is fun for Mark to watch Lucy explore. Lucy stops to look at everything she sees. If she gets too close to Mark's feet, Mark is very careful not to step on her.

Lucy can get stuck or squeeze herself into hiding places when she is out of her cage. Mark knows that if Lucy goes where he can't reach her, he can lure her back by holding a cardboard tube with a little food inside near her nose. And even if he sees her crawling into trouble, Mark never grabs her quickly, because he knows this will scare her.

Just before he goes to sleep,
Mark tells Lucy "Good night!"
And Lucy sometimes says
"squeak, squeak." Mark is glad
that he has a gerbil for a friend.